Dissections

poems by

Joanna Lee

Finishing Line Press
Georgetown, Kentucky

Dissections

for the broken ones

Copyright © 2017 by Joanna Lee
ISBN 978-1-63534-250-5 First Edition
All rights reserved under International and Pan-American Copyright Conventions.
No part of this book may be reproduced in any manner whatsoever without written permission from the publisher, except in the case of brief quotations embodied in critical articles and reviews.

ACKNOWLEDGMENTS

I am grateful to several magazines and their editors for publication of the following individual poems within this collection:

An earlier version of "Zingarella" was published in *Right Hand Pointing*

"field notes" was featured in Virginia Commonwealth University's *Medical Literary Messenger*

"chemistry lessons" was published in Yale Medical Group's *Caduceus*, Volume 10

"environmental studies" was featured (under the title "notes on the physiognomy of heart-break") by *Quail Bell* magazine

"there is a poem" was published by editor Lisa Zaran in *Contemporary American Voices*, and is also pending publication as part of *Their Own Bare Hands*: An Anthology of the 2015 Bridgewater International Poetry Festival

"the physiology of bursting" and "notes on cardiac physiology" are both Found poems written for and shared in the *ArtiPeeps* online community (https://artipeeps.wordpress.com)

Publisher: Leah Maines
Editor: Christen Kincaid
Cover Art: Joanna Lee
Author Photo: Elizabeth Bowie
Cover Design: Elizabeth Maines McCleavy

Printed in the USA on acid-free paper.
Order online: www.finishinglinepress.com
        also available on amazon.com

Author inquiries and mail orders:
Finishing Line Press
P. O. Box 1626
Georgetown, Kentucky 40324
U. S. A.

Contents

Zingarella 1
the physiology of bursting 2
we try to keep the doors shut 3
field notes 4
what we mean by *inquiet* 6
chemistry lessons 7
generation gap 9
ash & uncertainty 10
notes on cardiac physiology 12
notes on the county dump 13
what I found inside the black box 15
environmental studies 16
small mercies 17
there is a poem 18
antiseptically 20
reconstitution 22
Spring at Dad's 23
Tuesday 24

Zingarella[1] (if I had been born other than I had)

I'd write our song to gypsy music in dark bars on late weeknights, the wail of clarinets and accordions wielded by skinny-legged musicians vibrating through the cheap plastic seat and up into my bones. we'd sit picking the scabs of the past with oily fingertips, thinking there is resonance here somewhere, the candle-lit southpawed slant of scrawl running parallel to words I wouldn't understand. like when you said *some things have to change.* like when the lead singer called her a heartbreaker, and I remember I said *break* is really not the right word. hearts aren't like porcelain. they're all muscle and mallow. if I were to pluck yours out of its wet cavity and throw it, beating, on the empty dance floor, it might even bounce.

---

[1] Title of a love song as interpreted by My Son the Doctor at The Camel, Richmond, Virginia.

the physiology of bursting

a threshold is not a point
down-river,
a huge handless clockface
formed by stone-remembered
rooms full of whispering
glass. test the walls,
no matter how close.
the thick, white-
tiled passages
converge like
fast current: rapt &
rusted. lightwells hold
to the saddle,
to the boundary defining
a patient shadow
cleaning a window full
of the damp footfall'ed equilibria
who refuse to leave.
if the precise initial condition
is a cradle's pulse,
small perturbations
will certainly push
the limit cross grimed flags
to one side or the other.
find the keyholes.
dust the hinges.
walk spiking
and of great length. glow.

found from
The Bridge by Iain Banks
and
Dynamical Systems in Neuroscience: The Geometry of Excitability and Bursting by Eugene M. Izhikevich. Section 4.3.2: "Stable/Unstable Manifolds"

we try to keep the doors shut

fleeting as the dust left on palms
    after the gentle crush
of a moth against the cream
canvas of walls   stained yellow with lifetimes
of nicotine, nothing   as fragile as a poem

will ever bear the weight
    of my father's eyes.

        hardest to see is how he slows,

resigned, and I wonder if loneliness
is something inherited, something bred
    among the wildflowered fields
and splattered-animal byways of my youth,

    and his youth, among the mists   of red June mornings
starred with Queen Anne's lace,

        the blue-shadowed valleys
growing green with the blood of so many young lifetimes
and why, after a night of quiet drinking   and staring
    blankly at constellations we both wish we could name,

there are not enough words to fill
the space of leaving, and no medicine
I will ever learn   to bring back the limb missed
since childhood,
    father, this is the only healing I know.

field notes

I think I am in love
with little plastic needles, sterile
blues, the arrogance
of early a.m. overhead
lighting; size 6 latex
gloves that snap
to the thrill of a one-
handed knot
in 2-0 silk, over
and under
and over again;
back pockets
stuffed with blunt scissors &
stethoscope & note-
cards that read
like a map through
heartache:

the femoral nerve
courses laterally
to its artery as it passes
the triangle of Scarpa.
blood enters the liver
at 1500cc a minute,
mostly through the portal
vein, whose pressure
should not rise more than
5 millimeters of mercury
above the pressure
of other veins. once cardiac muscle
has ceased to contract,
it may be massaged
into restarting.

other things, too, I
knew, that I would have
learned harder
had I thought they
could save you.
some nights
I miss those mornings,
sunless & taped
into narrow tubing
with adhesive
that still pulls,
even now.

what we mean by *inquiet*

a name from memory,
sudden as whiskey, can stir
an almost particulate warmth,
slow dust spun to gold
in late afternoon light.
funny how things so disparate
sidle up: in late October
the red leaves from the playground
drift through gaps in the chain link
to gather among the graves.
we call this *neighborhood*,
the shawl-draped woman
walking her dog by the track's length,
disappearing behind a half-
felled oak as the sun shrinks
behind a cloud. the gray rows
huddle close, scripted
with their sad stories; the wind
pushes the swings in longing,
remembering the girl she maybe was.
on a good night, you can only *hear*
the gunshots. there are missing teeth
the size of a map where the fence
meets the dying trampled grass,
the dog shit someone has left
in the weed-pebbled gravel.
by the front gates, the sign reads
no thru traffic.

chemistry lessons

there is salt, and there is salt.
what's the difference,
my father asked me
at dinner, *between sea
salt and table?* and I said
sea salt is less strict, dad,

more complicated;
but I don't know if that's right;
don't know its bio-
chemical makeup, how late
it lets its daughters
out at night. chemicals aren't

all latch-key and angle, you know.
for instance, there are some in the brain
more sensitive to love
than to cocaine. I've heard this;
that, chemically, love is the most terrible
addiction. *crazy women need brave lovers,*

the poet said; this I know also
to be true; I've seen crazy.
but I don't know their chemistry, either:
not love *or* crazy. my professor
used to wear unmatched socks;
his eyes were the color of sea glass.

he taught the break-up of salts.
he told my father once I
was the most impressive he'd ever had.
I could have loved him, then,
but I was addicted to my own heart-
beat, rhythm less biochemical

than electric: a crazy drummer
in my head banging morse
code to my chest. I hope he is brave,
at least wears unmatched socks.
too much salt can fuck
it all up, cause heart-

ache. like breathing in sea glass.
how long can you hold your
breath underwater? my cousin
and I used to swim in the lake
by my grandparents' house,
catch turtles on cane poles

with bits of old bread.
the biggest one we dragged up
onto the shore, and my father
sliced her neck while
her jaws were clamped
onto the back handle of an old broom.

that was before I knew chemistry.
or love. or that guilt could be as addictive
as cocaine. I'm not sure if this
is true, but I have seen crazy.
turtles, the poet said, *turtles
all the way down.*

generation gap

The sky is closer here, a heavy blue
like autumn waters before a storm.
Snaggled sunshine shakes off rock
salt residue from snow that didn't come,
breathes the frost-dusted fields into
Kodachrome color. She went to school
amid these valleys, high walls all around.
Fill more of your life with sky, she said,
touching my wrist with the tips of
wingless hands. She knew:
self-hate stings like a bad sunburn,
but it can't last. *Love is a sneaky character,*
she would say, seeing me cast my lips
at the door, tannic & twisted & hopeful.
I wonder if she ever made that list,
of things that move forward: seasons; waters;
time; pages; selves? If, seeing my January,
she would have cried: new year's day on a pale
shore littered with empty mermaid's purses
—shark egg sacs abandoned if not hatched—
unimportant which we call them;
the metaphor, for me, the same.

ash & uncertainty
> *(delta x times delta rho is greater than or equal to Planck's constant divided twice)*

There is no equation
for the exact

swirl of river
caressing the rocks

over Indian December
forevers, no formula

for the disembodied
hours disregarding any

linear concept of space-
time & becoming seconds

as the herons stalk
sunlight the way

you stalk my truth
with your fingers.

Some boy-faced
physicist

at the beginning
of last century,

in love with in-
quiet, proved

nothing
could be proven

with absolute
certainty. He

told the Schutzstaffel so
when they called him

White
Jew, went

on to work with
uranium, believed

in complicated
relationships.

When he died
(cancer),

three years before
the thought of me

was made possible
to trouble

the river-seeking
hands of you,

they marched from
the Kaiser's Institute

and lit candles
by his front door:

God,
mathematicians & all.

notes on cardiac physiology

hung with bedpans and hussars' sabres the human heart
has a discriminative touch.

mottled scarlet, it routes a solitary pathway
across continents, Oceans, losses.

the profound shores of forehead, scalp, tongue
are excitatory ghosts bowed by sorrows,

safari trophies that include the entire body
of its dark.

The stuffed polar bear at its entrance stands yards tall.

it receives different blood by moment, tastes
red of serotonin, is spared no-man's-land

by the lacrimal tearing of vessels.
it is intractable. it is artist. it is acute,

an arctic gag reflex with a visceral
trajectory but no position sense.

known to be a major circuit,
its fibers course through copper battles,

and may produce pain.

Found from
Neuroanatomy: An Atlas of Structures, Sections, and Systems, Fifth Edition, Sections 7-3 to 7-8: "Sensory Pathways" by Duane E. Haines,
and
The Rings of Saturn by W.G. Sebald

notes on the county dump

There is a break from the terrible heat
but still   a ban on burning, so we
turn round & round the yard,
piling the deadwood of accumulated storms
into the back of the pickup
until we are sick of it, the sack-like clothes
we wear to cover our bruises
sticking to arms & legs & backs
and there is a veritable bonfire's worth
in the shiny bed. Next

morning, we rise early & head
out, take the back road
to the county dump, its lands manicured
more neatly than the scrapes
of my fingers; we are only
a few miles out of town, the same
where, as a youth, I dreamed so often of escape,
my best friend and I on the library steps,
chewing summer pomegranate seeds
that became, years later, the seeds of poems.

There are slots here
for every kind of forgotten,
& for each slot, snowshovels, rakes, brooms.
Like the past is a parking space
you can back your truck right up to
& tip cleanly into the emptiness of myth.
Like by plucking every dead twig
from the soft ground, we can unmake the storm.
I didn't call her, my best friend,
that night when the winds came down.

They say Larry Levis[1] read his last
at that same library on a spring day.
Some poems are born of sweat
no cry for help can lessen. Alone,
we trace the progression
of hurt   from red, to midnight,
to the yellow of sunshine that sinks,
like a sad tattoo, into the regret
of our bodies. Even summer
doesn't slow   for us, anymore.

[1] www.blackbird.vcu.edu/v14n2/features/levis_handley/handley_page.shtml

what I found inside the black box

so much
can happen in a decade. in a night filled
with spiral-sta(i)red decline. things

to hold on to, in sacred letters tall as a man:
to touch. you should have known
there: *tangere*, like want. *volare*, to fly.

I've forgotten the past tense.
plusquamperfect *amaveram*,
but only in the wrong tongue. she died.

now that coat hangs hung, like a wish,
starched with thin veins, so much in a decade.
some things you grip against forever,

memoryclamped. what if you *could* fly,
glasseyed and steady? beads tight round
white wrist, to want with small fingers.

something many-touched to hang on to
in the night. meant to hold not to cut, meant
to hold not to cut. meant to hold not to cut.

environmental studies

I strung my heart from the strong arms of a joshua tree
to dry in the mojave sun.
It grew beautiful for a moment,
beautiful as all the poetry in the world.

>The veins tightened and cracked,
>muscle fibers stiffened and swung
>ever so slightly in the rarefied air,
>paling against the blue blue of the desert sky.

Sooner or later all things in the desert turn
to dust or stone and fall silent.
I let my heart to drink from bleached desert ground,
its fingers spread out among lonelinesses

>And I sank down, shallowly, to absorb
>the lesson of heat and sky:
>it must become harder
>to breathe before it becomes softer.

small mercies

Three blocks from the medical school,
there's a bar with the best cocktail in town.
Your eyes in your glass,
you paint me the autopsies
of infants, the politics of tissue
recovery while
I watch the bartender
—short, dark-haired— cut
apart the plastic from a six-pack,
believing, maybe, in its choking
hold on unlucky marine life.
We were all born underwater,
and things *do* get lost in the low light.
Looking out away from the hospital,
at the manicured turf patio, it's hard
to believe anatomists still haunt these grounds.
Poor, apparently, is the new postbellum. Sweeping
the sweat back from his bangs,
he slides us both another. I can't
taste the brand of the bourbon, but,
savoring the char of the rosemary's
smoke, we all three know
it's been one helluva century.
Later, dropping you by your car
in the parking lot-turned burial ground-
turned parking lot again, what I'll remember
is the pretty, marbled veins of the bartop,
is how he cut apart each goddamn ring
with a white-handled knife,
is the evening CSX rumbling overhead,
hard by the overpass, coal
unslowed in darkness, salt-rimmed.

there is a poem

in the exquisite onslaught
of early May traintracks,
late night rainstorms; swooning

plumes of cavalry. little
girl tips back a big bottle, up,
up. we compare commit-

ments, strawberries. I was
committed, once. it was
raining then, too. barefoot.

no white horses. no
pink rose. like the bathscents
I brought mother that

last time: rose, pink, bottle.
she never usedthem. this poem
is supposed to be

about other things, not
mothers and bottles: thunder,
the whistle of trains

in darkness. skipping
over rocks. barefoot
rivers can be

dangerous: no
white horses there,
either. it is

early May after all: who
will catch you? strawberry-
blonde, he called her.

she wrote him lovepoems
but even they were not
happy. fuck happy poems,

she tells me. poetry
is always barefoot. even
over broken glass.

antiseptically

                                          all ee-Rs look a-
                       like: the slow unravel of anxiety punc-

                                  tuated by adrenaline's red
                                    gloved hands. the floors

                               some catsick formica brand
                                        of bland break-

                              fast: wheat or oat-flecked
                              yellow-green: the color of

                                      stale love. the sheets
                                  are ghostly and rough,

                                remind me of absence,
                       of lost summers embroidered

                                        in goosebumps.
                                      it's like midnight,

              or 2 ay-em, slumped and slow-
                            headed, even at eleven

in the morning. the blood is too
bright. the fluorescence

too kind, the ceilings
too low. there is always

someone coughing,
and every 5 minutes or so,

a laugh. in whispers
we stitch together the broken-

ness of the day, hold
our lives clutched close

against the sterile smell,
waiting. I am never

dressed for it, but
god, it feels like coming

home.

reconstitution

if I took
your hardened winter's heart

and sliced
it thin enough

to bury deep
in the shallow cracks

of our bedroom
windows where

the rain leaves
lonesome drips

down cold cream walls,
would the pieces swell like sponges

and soak up the sadness
that seeps between us

like a future
without a future

?

Spring at Dad's

The new green does nothing to tame them:

plane after plane engines over, a litany
of small-town boys who never graduated
to the Lear jets of their day school dreams.

We spend the time sifting
the leaffall of years from a hard warm
earth, clearing the way for the grass

my mother wanted so badly,
all her wheelbarrows of dirt,
all her fingernails & unshakable cough of dirt.

The irises in the canopy beds begin
to lift their heads and shrug off sleep;
Easter lilies already slumping to ground.

The falling pollen catches like powdered sugar
on the down of my forearms, like
the dust on her jewelbox, like the days

from that May morning when she
left breath behind and we
woke up yet a part of the flight path.

Tuesday
(Je dirai les mots, les poèmes[1])

it's just a poem, he says.

& he doesn't ask about my day, but I
tell him, regardless, that
I've been listening
to the same song
I've been listening

to all week, that,
after much deliberation, I've decided
it's in french: *Aïcha,*
Aïcha, écoute-moi, and I
don't speak any french, but

I'm reading a *Journal*
piece about Bellevue
during that big storm; how
10 million gallons of seawater
were pumped from its

basement[2], how
the lights went, ultimately,
out. *écoute-moi.* I've plugged
in the christmas tree, note
the needles on the floor.

---

[1] all italicized lyrics in French are from *Aïcha*, as performed in French & Arabic by Cheb Khaled, written by Jean-Jacques Goldman, 1996.
[2] "The Storm and the Aftermath," Danielle Ofri, M.D., Ph.D., *NEJM* vol 367, No.24. Dec 13, 2012.

would you like a love song?
he asks à la drive-thru
attendant, and I am done
with the housework now
& rolling cookie dough, wondering

while I flour if
attending a burlesque show
with a girl who likes me
would be pushing
the envelope, and staring

at my mother's handwriting
on the back of the recipe card,
which brings me back
to the mechanics
of hospitals and wondering

what it would be to push
an envelope down a dark
med-surg ward, IV
lines trailing like seaweed.
something like *Titanic*, maybe:

all fear and Atlantic sky.
enjoy your evening in peace,
he says, dreaming me in venus
while the violins play their last.
Moi, je ne veux que de l'amour.

the stars are out,
and here is no drowning.
in peace, he says. me,
I generally disbelieve
in poems with footnotes.

Never having formally studied English or creative writing past high school, **Joanna Lee** instead focused on the sciences, earning her MD from the Medical College of Virginia in 2007 and a further Master's Degree in Applied Science (neuroscience) from the College of William and Mary in 2010; her writing life focuses particularly on the overlap of creativity and healing.

Joanna's poetry has been published in a number of online and print journals, including *Rattle, Caduceus, Floodwall,* and *The Dead Mule School of Southern Literature,* and has been nominated for both Best of the Net and Pushcart prizes. A leading force behind Richmond's River City Poets, Joanna teaches workshops and makes possible a wide range of literary happenings from Shockoe Slip to South of the James. She is currently serving as Board Chair of the James River Writers, and lives in Richmond's Northside with her fiancé John and their cat Max.

www.ingramcontent.com/pod-product-compliance
Lightning Source LLC
LaVergne TN
LVHW050046090426
835510LV00043B/3331